FATHERHOOD

IS NOT FOR BABIES

*Becoming the Kind of Father
You Really Want to Be*

Emma S. Etuk, Ph. D

Emida International Publishers
Washington, DC - Uyo, Nigeria

Fatherhood
Is Not For Babies

Becoming the Kind of Father
You Really Want to Be

by

Emma S. Etuk, Ph. D

Text copyright © 1997 by Emma S. Etuk
Cover design by Fred LaPlant
Book design and typesetting by
Proclaim Publishing
proclaim@usa.net

Emida International Publishers
P.O. Box 50317
Washington, DC 20091

For additional copies, contact the address above.
Emida International Publishers is a division of
Emida International Services, Inc.

ISBN: 1-881293-01-7
Printed in the United States of America

Dedicated to

ALL FATHERS

who are faithfully endeavoring to make their
lives exemplary for their children and
their children's children.

Fatherhood

Is Not For Babies

Becoming the Kind of Father
You Really Want to Be

ACKNOWLEDGMENTS

The birth of my daughter, Ememobong, in 1989 and my son, Iniobong, in 1994, has given me the joys and experience of fatherhood. Simply, babysitting both of them has been all education, indeed. I have actually learned that, perhaps, the greatest gift a father can give to his children is time. Children really demand our availability. From my two children, I am grateful for this understanding.

I am also grateful to the Reverend Stephen K. Gyermeh, the senior pastor of the Church of the Living God, Hyattsville, Maryland, who, in 1992, first opened his pulpit for me to address the lively congregation on this subject. The enthusiastic reception of that address convinced me that there was really a need to reach a wider audience.

In the same vein, I am thankful to the Reverend Justiniano Cruz of the Alpha Omega Full Gospel Church for the opportunity to address the Hispanic community on this matter.

I wish also to thank Dr. Stephen Olford, the dean of American expository preachers, who graciously read the manuscript. Dr. Olford's Encounter Ministries over ELWA have been an inspiration to me for many years.

For a brief period, I was attending the Washington Community Fellowship where I was well fed with the word from the powerful preaching of Dr. Myron S. Augsburger. I thank him for his encouragement and for reading the manuscript.

The same kind of admiration and thanks are due to Dr. Robert B. Smeltzer, of the United Methodist Church, Dr. Corinthia Boone, founder of the Together in Ministry International, and to my buddy and countryman, Dr. Nseobong G. Utuk, founder of the Word of Faith Ministries.

Also, I want to thank some friends who gave financially toward this work. I prefer not to mention their names in order not to embarrass them.

Finally, I must thank Ayda, my precious wife, for her continuous support and faith in my dreams, without which it would be difficult to achieve this particular success.

May the reading of this book be a blessing to all the fathers and families that are struggling in a world that is increasingly becoming fatherless. To God be all the glory.

Emma S. Etuk, 1997

CONTENTS

FOREWORD

Why Another Book on Fathers?

It was during the hot summer months of June, 1992 and I had just graduated five weeks earlier from Howard University's Graduate School. Two congregations in the Washington, DC metropolitan area asked me if I would like to speak to them on the next Father's Day. I thought to myself: "What would I say to them?"

Three years before, I had become a father of a little, most precious and most beautiful girl whom we call Ememobong, nicknamed Mimi. Since then, I had gained some experience on fathering, though certainly not an expert. But, I had not expected that so soon I would be requested by anybody to speak on the subject.

In our contemporary rat-race to succeed, fathering is not often taught to prospective fathers. Fathering is not an easy thing. According to William Reynolds, the author of *The American Father: A New Approach to Understanding Himself, His Woman, His Child* (1978), "being a father in America's consumer-minded society is not a glamorous image, nor, for that matter, does it bring forth even a sparkle in a world which seems to value visibility above all else." [1]

Every father today knows, even instinctively, something of the helplessness associated with fathering. Nancy R. Gibbs of *Time* magazine (1993) has written that "the message dads get is that they are not up to the job. And a record number don't stick around-- even as fathers are needed more than ever." [2]

Many men are often scared to death when a woman utters those frightful word, "Honey, I'm pregnant." In my case, I was not scared. I was overripe for fathering. I had never had a child, and I was over forty years old.

In my upbringing, I had some strong religious beliefs about fatherhood. Our family was one in which my father was present and mother was loyal. We obeyed my dad and respected him. [3] We had family morning prayers nearly every day. Dad led those prayers. I thought I had some good ideas on fatherhood. But, when I was asked to publicly address this subject, I suddenly felt inadequate and needed some resources for preparation to speak at the churches.

Soon, I discovered that very little had been written or said on the matter of fatherhood. Sociologist Vaughn Call, who heads the National Survey of

Families and Households at the University of Wisconsin, is quoted as saying that research studies have produced "scant idea how many fathers there are [in America] . . . There's no interest in fathers at all . . . It's a nonexistent category. It's the ignored half of the family." [4]

There are about seventy million mothers between the ages of fifteen and older in the United States today, according to a recent *Time* magazine account. Who knows how many fathers there are? According to Ken R. Canfield, founder of the National Center on Fathering in Kansas, "5.6 million children under the age of fifteen are growing up without fathers." [5]

The recent interest in fatherhood may be credited to Bill Cosby, the celebrated African-American comedian whose two books, *Fatherhood* (1986) and *Childhood* (1991) have heightened our awareness of the subject. *Fatherhood* was an instant best-seller.

As my bibliography at the end of this book shows, there are nearly three dozen books in the literature. But, more perplexing is the fact that few of these books are written from a Christian perspective. They have little spiritual emphasis.

Many of the available books are, therefore, heavily secularized. Others are works with a sociological or psychological orientation. It is difficult to find a good book on fatherhood that is written from a biblical standpoint and which teaches what a father ought to be, or what he should do in preparation for the onerous task of fathering. Whatever has been discussed on this subject is buried in the many books on the general issues of marriage and the family.

For example, the book, *Climbing Jacob's Ladder* (1992) by the distinguished University of Maryland Professor, Andrew Billingsley, deals with the "common myths and misinformation about the black family." [6]

However, it has nothing to say about the biblical message to all fathers, or to the black father in particular. A person who goes to this book searching for a spiritual answer to the problems of the African-American families will be disappointed. *Climbing Jacob's Ladder* is a good place to start, though.

The Measure of a Man: Becoming the Father You Wish Your Father Had Been (1993) by Dr. Jerrold Lee Shapiro is the most comprehensive book on the subject which I have read. Like Billingsley's book, this book has no biblical nor scriptural foundation. But, it is very, very useful. What is lacking in Shapiro's book has been provided for in the essay, "The Meaning of Fatherhood" by Claude L. Dallas, Jr. in *Men to Men: Perspectives of Sixteen African-American Christian Men* (1996) by Lee N.

June and Matthew Parker. Mr. Dallas' insights are drawn from his Christian experience.

The cynicism of the secular press and the media is reflected in the sentiments expressed by Nancy Gibbs when she writes that, "Fatherhood is fragile and needs to be encouraged by the society around it." [7]

It is my belief that the type of encouragement which Gibbs calls for must include a spiritual dimension. So far, modern men and women have acted as if fatherhood lay outside the realm of religious influences. And, surely we have been reaping the harvest from such a perspective.

This book on fatherhood is an attempt to fill a particular void. Because there are not many books with a Christian perspective on fatherhood, and because those that are available lack a spiritual emphasis, I have written this book. It is my hope that it will be an asset to many men and women, families, and persons engaged in the area of Christian work.

I have particularly in mind all the young men who are asking the great and important questions: "What does the Bible say about fathers?" "How do I know that God is interested in me as a father?" "What are the requirements for fatherhood?" "What are the responsibilities of fathers?" "What are the rewards for fatherhood?" "How can I be sure that I will be successful as a father in today's difficult world?"

I intend to follow closely the lines of my sermon delivered on June 21, 1992 to the Church of the Living God and to the Hispanic Mennonite Church, both in Hyattsville, Maryland.

I intend to keep the discussion as lively (and still as serious) as it was on that hot summer day at both congregations. I hope that the reader will be blessed as much as the people in those two congregations were blessed. And, I honestly pray that this book will contribute to the spiritual and social well-being of the families in America and throughout the world today.

INTRODUCTION

Bill Cosby, in his characteristic and humorous manner wrote, some years ago, that father hood is asking your son to make up a name rather than tell anybody whose son he really is.[1] George Herbert stated that a "Father's Day is like Mother's Day, except [that] the gift is cheaper."[2]

On a more serious note, Cosby added, "It is easy for a father to say that a child who will not behave is not his problem but the problem of the boss of the house, his wife." "Real fatherhood," he insisted, "means total acceptance of the child for better or worse . . ."[3] At the time that Bill Cosby wrote these words, he had five children. So, he knows what he is talking about. As many fathers will discover, fathering demands on the job training.

To raise five children in our contemporary world is no easy task, especially in America. You must buckle up your belt if you want to be a successful father. If you want to raise good children, be prepared for hard work. A good child, the Bible tells us, is a mother's joy and a father's pride. Also, remember this: "The glory of children are their fathers" (Prov. 17:6).

Our modern world has many problems. I believe that one of the crises of our modern society is this: there are too many liliputians walking around and parading themselves as fathers. These are people who have never really grown up, matured. They were never ripe to become fathers. They are like apples plucked with their acid content for consumption. Such apples are never sweet but often bitter.

Very unfortunately, we live in a time that may be best described as the age of fatherly puerility--babies making babies and being proud of it! Generally, when the term "father" and its derivative "fatherhood" are mentioned, one readily thinks of procreation, which is the sexual aspect of fatherhood.

Fatherhood involves much more than having sexual intercourse. It is more than bringing a child into this world. There are many creatures that pro-create but they are not fathers.

Certainly, an important aspect of fatherhood is its procreative characteristic. But, listen again to Bill Cosby who has said that "having a child is surely the most beautifully irrational act that two persons in love can commit."[4] When you do that, he adds,

You've decided to give up quiet evenings with good books and lazy weekends with good music, inti-mate meals during which you finish whole sentences, sweet private times when you've savored the thought that just the two of you and your love are all you will ever need. You've decided to turn your sofas into trampolines, and to abandon the joys of leisurely contemplating reproductions of great art for the joys of frantically coping with reproductions of yourselves.[5]

Because of our preoccupations with only the procreative aspects and processes of fatherhood, we have produced men who are sexually intoxicated. In America today, fatherhood is highly sexualized. And children, the dear products of our procreative endeavors, have become the unpleasant casualties of our free-for-all, insatiable, sexual appetites. Fatherhood is not for babies. It is for mature adults.

There are three other aspects of fatherhood that must constantly be kept in mind. These are: a biblical doctrine on fatherhood, a biblical style of fatherhood, and the perseverance needed for successful fatherhood. Without these three elements, fatherhood can center upon the animalistic instinct alone. These three aspects will be discussed in the next chapters.

I suppose that this situation, of seeing fatherhood only in its sexual aspect, is the popular one today. I am alarmed at the lack of frequent instruction from the pulpits on what it takes to be a father. Because of this lack of godly and fruitful education, our "young

American males [have become] our biggest national tragedy. Males between the ages of eighteen and twenty-five are the real cause of our crime problem."[6] Our teenage males have bought the lies of the secular press and media which constantly bombard them with the "if it feels good, do it" message.

Let me present to you the picture as it is today. According to a special report on the state of the black American family by *Newsweek* magazine titled, "A World Without Fathers: The Struggle to Save the Black Family" and published on August 30, 1995, "Two out of three first births to black women under 35 are now out of wedlock."[7] This report continues to say that

In 1960, the number was two out of five, and it's not likely to improve any time soon. A black child born today has only a one-in-five chance of growing up with two parents until the age of 16 . . . The impact, of course, is not only on the black families but on all of society. Fatherless homes boost crime rates, lower educational attainment and add dramatically to the welfare rolls.[8]

A black mother named Caballero, in New York City, is said to come from three generations of a fatherless home and fears that her own granddaughter "is destined to be the fourth generation in her family to raise a child without a man."[9] Reading something like this ought to cause all the preachers to squirm; but do they?

A study by James Patterson and Peter Kim revealed that one-fourth (i.e., 54 million) of all Americans claimed that they best can be described as "sexually insatiable."[10] It is no wonder then that the sexual abuses of children are rampant.

Another media report stated that 62 percent of all black children in America are born out of wedlock. Fifty-five percent of these are born by women who have never been married. Sixty-seven percent of all black families is said to be headed by single women.[11]

Like Caballero in the *Newsweek* account, I ask, "Where are the men?" "Where are all the fathers of all these children?" They have taken their leave!

Patterson and Kim concluded their study with these sobering words: "In America, sex is an obsession"[12] and "sex, for the majority of Americans, is available for the asking."[13]

Living in the United States for over a decade, I have personally observed this trend. I maintain that the ignorance of and the disobedience to the biblical injunctions on fatherhood have led to the trivialization of the holy sacrament of marriage and of the family.

The Holy Bible is not entirely silent on the subject of fatherhood.[14] We should understand that the authors of the sixty-six books of the Bible were generally persons who held very high views about the family, marriage, sex and fatherhood. In the New Testament, these authors were either the apostles of Jesus Christ or were persons closely associated with the followers of Jesus Christ. Eight of them, including the author of the book of the Hebrews, wrote the twenty-seven books of the New Testament.

One of the eight authors was John Zebedee whose perspective on fathers I will analyze later. The other seven were Matthew, Mark, Luke, Paul, Peter, James, and Jude. None of them, I say, had any of the foolish ideas about fatherhood and motherhood which we find prevalent and acceptable today. If we care to acknowledge it, our idea of fatherhood goes a long way back into biblical history. The next chapter is about this biblical history and doctrine.

1

A BIBLICAL DOCTRINE
ON FATHERHOOD

Marriage is the cornerstone of the family and of any society. Whatever happens to it affects society. If marriages are rotten, society will be also. If families have experiences of disharmony, society will also be affected. Thus, if men and women are at each other's throat, the children are bound to suffer. We must, therefore, return to the Bible to discover God's order for the family. There, we will also discover the Word of the Lord for fathers

The Scriptures say that in the beginning God created men and women (Gen. 1:27). The term "father" appears early in the Scriptures, in Genesis chapter two verse 24. In Genesis chapter three verse 20, the text implies that Adam was a husband. Soon, he became a father and had Cain and Abel as sons (Gen. 4:1-2).

The Scriptures also teach that "children are an heritage of the LORD: and the fruit of the womb is his reward" (Ps. 127:3). The secular view of the family is that in which the child is merely property. The biblical view is that in which every child is a gift from God and the child is very precious in God's sight.

The man is the head of the family; the wife is his loyal partner; and the children love, respect, and obey their parents (I Cor. 11:3). This biblical view has no room for the contemporary view of man which seems to be hostile and antagonistic. It has nothing to do with current notions of feminism which often seems to pitch the man against the woman. God is deeply interested in the family, in marriage, and in fathers.

John Zebedee, mentioned earlier, wrote the following words: "I write unto you, fathers, because you have known him who is from the beginning" (I Jn. 2:13-14). The *Amplified Bible* reads thus: "I write to you, fathers, because you have come to know (recognize, be conscious of, and understand) Him who (has existed) from the beginning." Here, John Zebedee is referring to the opening words of the Scriptures (Gen. 1:1) and Jn. 1:1-3).

John Zebedee was following in the footsteps of his master. Once, when Jesus was questioned about the institution of marriage, he took his audience back to the beginning. There, at the beginning, we find what was God's mind for fathers, for mothers, and for the family. John seems to remind his audience that the best place to start a walk as fathers is by the acknowledgment of our God who created us, who has always existed from the beginning, and who supplies us with all the wonderful blessings of this life.

This implies that we cannot function well without Him. We cannot be atheists, polytheists, pantheists, materialists, or even naturalists who have assumed our autonomy. The simple acknowledgment of the existence of God and His lordship over us releases our spirit to praise and adore Him as the provider of the children which we have. This spiritual release also enables us to seek His wisdom in the onerous task of fathering.

As I said earlier, children are God's precious gifts to us. Every child has a father. There are no bastards but God's little, innocent and wonderful creatures who are often mistreated and abandoned by sinful men and women. Every child, therefore, needs a father, a good father, to take care of God's wonderful gift.

The one requisite to becoming a good father is to be linked to the great Father above through a spiritual metamorphosis. The way to this metamorphosis is faith in His son, Jesus Christ, who is the glorious expression of God's image and character. In the New Testament, the apostle Paul took time to expose the qualities of Jesus.

We can note the following seventeen qualities from Paul in Colossians 1:13-29:

1. Jesus is God's dear son (v. 13).

2. Jesus has a kingdom (v. 13).

3. Jesus provides redemption (v. 14).

4. Jesus provides forgiveness (v. 14).

5. Jesus is the image of God (v. 15).

6. Jesus is the firstborn of every creature (v. 15).

7. Jesus created all things (v. 16).

8. Jesus owns all things (v. 16).

9. Jesus had a pre-existence (v. 17).

10. Jesus holds all things together (v. 17).

11. Jesus is the head of the Church (v. 18).

12. Jesus rose from the dead (v. 18).

13. Jesus is pre-eminent (v. 18).

14. Jesus is the fullness of God (v. 19).

15. Jesus provides real peace (v. 20).

16. Jesus is the reconciler of all things (v. 20-21).

17. Jesus is able to keep you to the end (v. 22).

Because of these unique qualities of Jesus, John Zebedee insisted that fathers get to *know* Him. I have studied those instances when John addresses a specific person(s). Examine the following:

1. little children (1 Jn. 2:1)

2. brethren (1 Jn. 2:7)

3. little children (1 Jn. 2:12)

4. fathers (1 Jn. 2:13)

5. young men (1 Jn. 2:13)

6. little children (1 Jn. 2:13)

7. fathers (1 Jn. 2:14)

8. young men (1 Jn. 2:14)

9. little children (1 Jn. 2:18)

10. little children (1 Jn. 2:28)

11. little children (1 Jn. 3:7)

12. my brethren (1 Jn. 3:13)

13. little children (1 Jn. 3:18)

14. beloved (1 Jn. 3:21)

15. beloved (1 Jn. 4:1)

16. little children (1 Jn. 4:4)

17. believers in God (1 Jn. 5:13)

In essence, John is writing to the believers, the brethren, and the beloved. When he uses the term "children" (eight times he does so), we should not think that he is referring to toddlers. He is writing to adults, to persons capable of being biological and spiritual fathers. He sees himself in the position of "the elder" brother, the oldest of the original disciples still alive. The other eleven had by then been martyred.

Ninety-eight times in his gospel, John uses the term "believe." But, in his letters, he moves a step further to talk about the *relationship* of an earthly father with his heavenly Father. Note verse three of 1 John 1. Here, John is showing us *the relational aspect of belief* (trust) in God.

Just as our heavenly Father and his son, Jesus Christ, believe or trust each other, there ought also to be a trusting relationship between an earthly father and the heavenly Father. Such a relational trust is rooted in a proper kind of knowing. You ordinarily would not trust someone you do not properly know, would you? Fathers ought, therefore, to know Christ

1. intimately,

2. affectionately,

3. passionately, and

4. intelligently.

Jesus taught much on the fatherhood of God. Indeed, it has been said that only in the Christian religion do we have a concept of God as our father. Think about this for a moment. Jesus referred to God as His father several times (Matt. 10: 32-33; Lk. 10:22; Jn. 5:17; 10:29-32). He taught us that God is our father, especially for those who trust Him (Matt. 6: 1-17).

In the famous prayer which Jesus taught His disciples, we are to pray to God who is our Father in heaven (Matt. 6:9). This, our good and caring heavenly father, allows His sun to shine for the good and the wicked. He sends rain to bless all His creation. He is liberal and good in His dealings with men and women. We learn also that He is loving, tolerant, patient, kind, and forgiving. These are the qualities that a father must have if he is to be a good father and parent.

It is in this manner that such fathers would transfer their spirituality to their children as commanded by Scripture (Prov. 22:6) which says that we must train up a child in the way that he must go, and when he is old, he would not depart from it. Because fathering is a very difficult work, earthly fathers need a relationship with God to help them succeed in this responsibility. They need a spiritual resource and this resource is at the heart of our morality, doctrine, and social engagement. Those without it, I dare say, do so at their peril. They soon will find that fatherhood is a frustrating human experience.

The Scriptures encourage us to count on God and on Christ for the proper upbringing of our children. God provided these children. We cannot afford to act as if we created them ourselves. We are merely God's stewards. Our responsibility is to act well on his behalf. We are to remember that we can receive his approbation or condemnation, depending upon how we treated the little, precious gifts He gave to us.

Fathers who love God and acknowledge Him will communicate this to their children. This is inevitable. God will see them through the hard task of fathering. The Bible says: "In all thy ways acknowledge him, and he shall direct thy paths" (Prov. 3:6). This promise includes the joyful and difficult task of fathering.

2

THE FOUR REQUIREMENTS OF FATHERHOOD

I now come to an area of this discussion of which many of today's young males are woefully ignorant. This deals with the practical preparations for fatherhood. In my judgment, fatherhood requires these four very important qualities:

1) physical maturity,

2) intellectual maturity,

3) financial maturity, and

4) spiritual maturity.

Physical Maturity

Young man, listen to me. Just because you can wear a pair of trousers does not make you a man any more than wearing make-up makes a girl a woman. This is only the superficial side of our being. I will be very blunt with you and say that just because you get a girl pregnant does not make you a man. A man is more than an ordinary, physical object who enjoys ordinary, physical pleasures.

Biology, and particularly zoology, teaches us a lot about our human physiology. William S. Beck, a medical doctor at Harvard University, writes that, "The human body, like other organisms, is an organized complex of materials and functions that operate together in ways that enhance survival of the individual organism and its species."[1] The body is a wonderful creation. David, the psalmist, said centuries ago that we are "fearfully and wonderfully made" (Ps. 139:14). We have a complex body that defies total human comprehension.

Our body must be nurtured and preserved in a way that it is not easily harmed or destroyed. A young man living in this age of venereal diseases, pollution and ecological disasters must be aware that he has only one body which he can call his own. Indeed, if he is a Christian, that body does not belong absolutely to him. It belongs to God.

Fatherhood starts with this knowledge: that the body is a precious gift from God. It is a wonderful machine. It functions and sustains us only if we treat it right. If we abuse it, we have grave consequences to bear. Those who have wantonly abused their bodies have regretful stories to tell.

I must solemnly warn all men that our reproductive organs are important areas of our body prone to all kinds of abuses and harm. The Bible clearly warns us against the abuse of our body. In this day of AIDS, it is not fun to sow our wild oats indiscriminately. A potential father must be sober over matters related to physical, sexual intercourse. It is not old-fashioned to say that a body takes years to mature and be ready for fatherhood. Promiscuity in the use of our body will affect that maturity. In the animal kingdom, babies do not make babies. Why are we human beings doing so?

Let the clarion call go forth to the young men of our generation that being a successful father involves allowing our bodies to grow, mature and be disciplined.[2] This is our insurance against bodily abuse, infection, insatiable sex, infidelity, divorce and pain. A healthy physical body is vital to successful fatherhood.

Intellectual Maturity

A United Negro College Fund slogan is, "A mind is a terrible thing to waste." I propose that every young person alive today should be advised to memorize that slogan. Many of them do not possess the right kind of knowledge about sex. Many of the contemporary intellectual notions about sex are derived from the hedonism of an aberrant form of Epicureanism.

In our time, this hedonism has been given the fullest expression by the "playboy" philosophy of the Western world. According to *Details* magazine, ours is the "Sex Generation."[3] Even the music which our young boys listen to is filled with lyrics which emphasize the "playboy" perspective of human sexuality.

Each time I walk into a bookstore, I am always amazed at the types of novels in vogue for our gullible public. There are few books--the Jane Austin type--which can be called classic. One has only to talk to any of these boys to hear the rotten language which they have borrowed from these popular novels. Saleable novels seem to be those intended for Hollywood! Who has not read *How to Make Love to a Woman and Satisfy Her All the Time*?

The language of these boys is vulgar and sometimes very offensive. How can they, who soon would become fathers, teach their sons and daughters any better? When the Bible is presented to them as archaic and irrelevant, is it any wonder that these boys are wading through life like a ship without a compass?

Bible knowledge is good education by itself. So said Alfred Tennyson. In it, we find these immortal word: "The fear of the Lord is the beginning of knowledge: but fools despise wisdom and instruction" (Prov. 1:7). Those who despise this intellectual source soon become foolish and destitute of wisdom.

It is important that we encourage these young people to study hard and be well prepared for the tough job of raising a family. A good education in hand can be good insurance against joblessness and poverty. In the United States, where racism and discrimination add to the burden of social problems facing a black man, as the authors of *Cool Pose* (1992) have asserted, [4] it is imperative that males be taught the necessity to strive for higher intellectual achievement.

During the 1992-1993 school year, I personally witnessed the problem among black males who go to college, not to study, but to "have fun." Somehow, many of them had lost faith in the benefits of the diploma, given the unemployment rate in the United States at that time. They had become disillusioned with college training. The society owes them the responsibility to re-invigorate their faith in the academic system.

The church, in particular, must abandon its often anti-intellectual stance and show the light. Ministers at the pulpits must show a good amount of respect for academics. The happiest people I know are those who know Jesus Christ as their personal savior and who have also acquired a sound education. It takes a lot of knowledge these days to be a good father.

There are many books to be read in preparation for fatherhood. There are many books to be read to your child before and when he or she is at the pre-school-age. There are assignments that will need to be done when the child starts first grade. A child needs a father's role model in this respect. And, the ignorant is the least qualified for these tasks.

Above all, it is incumbent upon fathers to possess a worldview by the time they become parents. Much of the make-up of such a worldview will come from an intellectual discipline and maturity.

Financial Maturity

Fathering involves the payment of bills, many bills. When our daughter was about to be born at the Georgetown University Hospital in northwest Washington, DC, we least expected a cesarean birth. Although we had some form of health insurance soon we were saddled with a mountain of medical bills which took more than a year for us to pay off.

My wife and I have since learned that having children in America is a luxury. We cannot afford it.

"There are no free lunches," Americans often say. This statement applies also to feeding your child. A father soon finds out that his savings are quickly depleted. Unfortunately, many would-be fathers do not even save for their medical bills. They have no real home for their baby. Many reside in ghettoes or "projects." They have no educational plans for their newborn child. They only hope that friends and the government will supply their needs. That, my friend, is simply living like an animal. Even animals make advance preparations for their babies!

Every would-be father must clearly understand that he is responsible for every child he brings into this world. He must be ready to provide for his child(ren). Even animals do so. Why not a man? I will elaborate on this matter in chapter three dealing with the responsibilities of fatherhood.

Fathers must be men who know how to manage money. They must learn how to budget and control the family income. They must learn how to be debt-free. They must be financially disciplined men. If they cannot control their wallets, who will entrust them with abundant wealth? They must learn how to invest in worthy causes and, hopefully, keep the money for the education of their children. In my society, the traditional Ibibio culture of Nigeria, these are a man's duties. These are the things that constitute manhood, no more and no less. It is a shame for a man to be a beggar.

Spiritual Maturity

In a sense, this entire discussion is about the spiritual preparations for fatherhood. Every time I hear of a case of family violence, for example, wife battering or child abuse, I know that it is a case of spiritual immaturity in the home.

Spiritual maturity is a mental, psychological and religious state whereby a man knows that he is ready to lead a family and guide such a family against disharmony. It is a state of peaceful co-existence by all the members in a particular family. Spiritual maturity begins with the development of character and a set of values.

Every father's personal character will be tested by the demands of patience, perseverance and love. There is no such thing as a trouble-free family. It is the art of crisis-management in the home which counts and saves a marriage. Every child has his or her ways of testing the character of the parents. Perhaps nothing else in this world tests us more than the demands of the home. I know from experience what I am talking about.

I have often confessed to my wife that I do not know why any rational man would want to have more than two or three children. Believe me, the attention which children need--reading to them, answering all their questions, guiding them across the street, putting them to bed, picking up all their toys at the end of each day, babysitting and playing with them (the list is endless)--puts so much of a burden upon a parent that no sane man would want to breed children whom he is not ready to care for. It is no wonder that some men and women have chosen not to have children after marriage.

But, whatever plans one may make for his family, such plans cannot exclude the moral and religious dimension. Whether one believes the Bible or not, a child's proper growth and development is directly proportional to the extent of the parent's moral life. The Bible says that we must train up a child in the way that he must go, and when he is old, he will not depart from it (Prov. 22:6). But, how can a father train up a child when he himself is spiritually bankrupt?

These four requirements for fatherhood are, therefore, important. Those who will neglect or reject them are directly, or indirectly, contributing to the demise of our society. We must ask God to help us if we lack any of these requirements. My prayer is that many fathers will accept these principles and adhere to them for their own good and for the good of their families.

3

THE FOUR RESPONSIBILITIES OF FATHERHOOD

D r. Lewis Yablonsky says that, "The most important role a man can play in his lifetime is that of becoming a father. Fatherhood is a man's link with the future."[1]

If being a father is one of the sweetest, most fulfilling and most wonderful blessings in this life, then such a blessing has its awesome responsibilities.

A father's preparation for fatherhood involves a readiness to be responsible in the following four areas:

1. a father's responsibility to himself,

2. a father's responsibility to his wife,

3. a father's responsibility to his children, and

4. a father's responsibility to his relatives.

Now, listen to me very carefully. Before you take care of any one else in this world, you must, as a father, take care of yourself, your wife, your children, and your relatives which may sometimes include your aged parents, in-laws, uncles and aunts. No one else has these responsibilities but you.

My tax dollars should not do it for you. And, if you are man enough to have brought a child into the world, then you should be man enough to provide for yourself, your wife, your children, and your relatives. After all, I did not share in "the fun" that you had and I should not. Why should my tax dollars be used for the support of the offspring that are the products of your having "fun"?

I do not care if it was by accident, by choice, or by consensus. Fathers, you are responsible for the human beings whom you voluntarily brought into this world. If you were to seek the permission of those innocent babies before bringing them into this earth, they probably would have asked you if you can afford it. Therefore, fathers who do not pay for their children's support ought to be ashamed of themselves.

Because many fathers have abdicated these responsibilities, I indict the men of this generation for the parental callousness which has led to the scandalous preponderance of unwed teenage mothers and pregnancies.

I also indict the men of this generation for the "playboy," "penthouse," and "hustler" philosophies which have contributed to the presence of millions and millions of unwanted and uncared-for children--children whose only crime is that they were born, children innocently suffering from unnecessary hardships because some nut decided to have a fling or some "fun" somewhere and sometime, without first considering the consequences.

God will hold you accountable for the daily cries and tears of these unfortunate children. It is criminal to hurt an innocent child by this act of neglect. Repent, and find your child(ren) today! Resolve that from this day forward, by God's help, you will care for your children. They are your responsibility.

Remember that before we pushed aside this responsibility over to the government, God had instituted the family structure for the protection of every newborn child. This is why I admire the extended family system in African culture. There, the child belongs also to the community and not exclusively to the parents as it is in the Western world.

Let us examine our four areas of responsibility in some detail:

A Father's Responsibility to Himself

The first step in this regard is that you resolve from this day forward that you will keep yourself pure (Ps. 119:9-11 and 1 Tim. 5:22).

Here are ten blessings of a pure life for you to consider carefully:

Purity

1. aids boldness of character,

2. aids confidence among our peers,

3. prepares us for leadership,

4. lacks regrets,

5. aids in having a clear vision in life,

6. pleases God,

7. confirms our Christian testimony,

8. aids the progress of the Church,

9. builds a strong society, and

10. is a necessary ingredient for living a satisfactory, fulfilling life.

My friend, think about these ten points. Can you and I afford to miss them simply because we so much want to enjoy a life of promiscuity? No! I know that down in your heart, you want the best out of life. The way to experience that is through repentance and confession. You must claim the merits of the finished work of Jesus Christ upon the cross and His power to assist you in this matter.

If, after all that I have written, you still must sow your wild oats, just remember that sex without love is hypocritical. And clearly, sex without love and commitment to responsibility is bad sex. Dr. Edwin Louis Cole warns us that, "We live in what has been called the 'era of the mediocre man,' meaning men want authority but not accountability."[2]

Therefore, women, do not let any man sweet-talk you into anything. If he ain't got it, he ain't worth it. And I do not mean only money here. I mean also physical, financial, spiritual, and intellectual maturity. Ladies, you must not aid men in the cheapening of your precious sexuality.

Cole has said that, "There would be no pornography to look at if there were no women who desired to flaunt their sexual prowess."[3]

Do not be seduced by the contemporary mindset which says: "If you've got it, flaunt it." This type of reasoning is borne out of an irresponsibility regarding what can happen to us because of our carelessness. Just as a man must watch himself and strive toward purity, you ladies must do the same. Remember, it is you who carry the babies for nine months and often get abandoned during or after delivery of your baby.

Men, take care of your body, soul and spirit. Do not neglect yourself (II Tim. 2:1-2, 15). Be a well-rounded adult who practices godliness (I Tim. 4:7). Here are ten important things that you can strive to be, as part of your responsibility to yourself.

Do yourself a favor and be an:

1. object of admiration (Eph. 5:33),

2. object of inspiration (I Tim. 3:4),

3. object of godly pride (I Tim. 3:4),

4. object of blessedness (Prov. 31:28),

5. object of trust (Prov. 31:11),

6. object of nobility (Prov. 31:23),

7. object of respect (Eph. 5:33),

8. object of heroism for your children (Prov. 6:32),

9. object of your spouse's respect and submission (Col. 3:18-21), and

10. object of dutifulness (Prov. 22:29).

Be a busy bee and not the lazy, yawning drone. For fathers may lay up wealth for their children and not the other way around (Prov. 13:22; II Cor. 12:14-15). Strive to be the best you can be. Be committed to a life of principle. And, when you feel that you have failed yourself, remember that there is nobody on earth who ever succeeded without failing several times. Try, try and try again. Don't give up. Quitters never win.

I believe that if the young people are been taught these ten principles before marriage, there would be less family failures.

A Father's Responsibility to His Wife

This responsibility involves husbandhood. Every Christian husband should study the following texts: Eph. 5:23-23; I Cor. 7:2; 11:3; and Col. 3:19. Many excellent books on the art of husbandhood ought to be written to educate men on how to care for their wives. Experienced and successful married men should also share their insights.

But, until then, a father must be responsible to his wife by giving of himself and of the best things that he has to give her. Remember:

- If you fail with your wife, your family
  will be in deep trouble.
- If you fail with your wife, your business
  can be ruined.
- If you fail in your marriage, your life
  can surely come to an end.

Many men have been broken irreparably because of a failed marriage. Be warned!

A word for the African male. As a father in the home, you must learn to assist your wife in the success of your home. I mean that you must learn to cook, clean and coddle her to rest from the chores that daily tax her strength. You must take her out on surprise "dates" from time to time. It is not a

Western thing to do so. It is the right thing. You must buy her flowers and shop for the good things that enhance her beauty and elegance.

If you have children, you must learn how to change the diapers. You must no longer hold to the antiquated and archaic African idea that housework is entirely a woman's business. Yes, it may have been so centuries ago, when few women went to school and there was only an agrarian economy to support families. But times have changed.

In our cash economy and wage system, you must be fooling yourself to expect your wife to work tirelessly from sun-up to sun-down as a slave and then provide good sex to you at night. '

As for the Hispanic male, there is no room for the "macho" spirit. You must babysit and help in the home. Your wife is not your slave but your loving partner. If you disobey these charges, you can only expect rebellion against your irresponsibilities, selfishness, frustration and divorce. It is your choice. Choose the right path and attitude. It is only fair to treat the mother of your precious children right. Your children will notice it and, hopefully, will practice it.

Again, listen to me very carefully, you men. If you want the respect of your wife, you must earn it the old-fashioned way. I am earnestly serious. I cannot stand the men who bully and batter their wives. Oh, yes, she may talk like a parrot. But that does not give you the right to batter and bruise her. If you hope to win her submission this way, you are terribly mistaken. Indeed, you batter yourself by battering her.

The Scriptures say that both of you are one flesh. You are beating yourself! Do not, therefore, be surprised at the results you get. Self-control and matured manliness are expected of you as a husband.

Would you encourage your sister to live with any man who beats her up all the time? Certainly not! I believe that you would even join forces with your sister to rout this brutalizer.

Why? Because you love your sister very much. You want to protect her. You should, therefore, love your wife and be willing to protect her, no less than you would your sister. She is yours.

Your sister actually belongs to some other man. But, your wife is the one that you've got, the one that you vowed to love and protect "in sickness and in health, in riches and in poverty, and for better or for worse."

You must earn her respect and never lose that respect. A marriage without a mutual respect is on the road to its demise. A word should be enough for a wise man.

A Father's Responsibility to His Children

Let me point you again to the word of God regarding a father's relationship with his children. The wise King Solomon wrote that, "the glory of children are their fathers" (Prov. 17:6).

Think about it. Are you the glory of your children? I urge you to study the following portions of Scripture: Eph. 6:4; Col. 3:21; Prov. 19:18; 22:6; 23:13-14; 29:15-17; and Deut. 6:7.

Here, let me direct your attention to a few practical matters.

A father must be a role model, a mentor, a friend, and should display a Christlike example to his children. He should not be ashamed to apologize to his children when he is in error. He should be ready to ask for their forgiveness when he offends them. Man, you are not perfect. So, why pretend to your children that you are?

My friend, Dr. Matthew Sadiku, a Professor of Electrical Engineering at Temple University in Philadelphia, Pennsylvania, has published one of the best books on the family titled, *Secrets of Successful Marriages* (1991) in which he insists that a father must provide the following three things for his children:

1. authority in the home,

2. religious guidance in the home,

3. leadership in the home.[5]

I should add a fourth, namely, the provision of discipline in the home.

Today's children tend to want everything all at once, and their parents condone this behavior. They want toys, money, cars, sex, fun, and so on. It takes a strong and disciplined father to say "No" and "Enough" to his children these days.

Some parents have the erroneous idea that the supply of all kinds of gadgets to their children will make them good kids.[6] No, Sir! Your child may actually be spoiled by the superfluity of your "generosity." You may inadvertently be setting up your child for a lifestyle of greed. Your child may be developing a false sense of material things.

Experience has taught my wife and me that what a child needs most is our <u>time</u> and <u>availability</u>. Your child would call upon you even if you were President Bill Clinton holding an emergency meeting of the National Security Council (NSC). You are his or her father. And, that is all that the child cares about. You belong absolutely to him or her. And, he or she is right.

Once that child begins to feel that you no longer care, or that your unconditional love no longer exists, or that you have no time for him or her; in short, that he or she can no longer count upon you, or trust you for protection, you are finished. You might as well consider yourself childless.

This is the tragedy of many homes today. Parents have room or time for every other thing under the sun but for their precious little ones. Many nights, I am sickened by the sight of our black kids loitering about the neighborhoods and on the streets with no one to care. Where are their fathers? Is it any wonder that such children fall prey to pedophiles and child abusers?

Fathers, be available for your children. Sing to them before they go to sleep. Read to them. Pray with them. Teach them by example. Never tell your child to do the wrong thing. Set high standards for them.

Your children are full of energy and want to conquer the world. Help them to aim high. Leave the rest to a loving God who cares for your children much more than you do. He will see you through. Hallelujah. Praise the Lord!

A solemn word. Men, and preachers in particular, I must warn you about the Eli-like fathers in our society. Eli, a prophet of God in ancient Israel, allowed his children to grow up as ruffians in his parsonage. God warned him of his neglect to thoroughly discipline his children. He was too weak to correct them. Like our modern apostles of "no spanking," he spared the rod and pleased his children.

Eli's boys went as far as to have sexual intercourse with the women who came to worship. They did their own thing without any parental rebuke. Their father condoned these rapes on decency and morality. Sick of the mess, God pronounced judgment through the young prophet, Samuel (I Sam. 2:12 - 3:1-21 and 4:13-22). Eli represents the tragedy of a failed fatherhood.

The Scriptures have room for parental discipline. Do not be afraid of the irreligious, "liberal" ideas of the experts who say that you must not spank your child. Believe the biblical admonition which says, "He that spareth his rod hateth his son: but he that loveth him chasteneth him betimes" (Prov. 13:24). I must add that spanking must be corrective and in love, not out of anger, vengeance or hatred which in turn will result in abuse and bruises.

A father must always keep in mind the biblical injunction to, "Train up a child in the way that he must go: and when he is old, he will not depart from it." This admonition involves, first of all, <u>instructional</u> discipline rather than <u>punitive</u> discipline. Never punish a child until you have instructed your child. Otherwise, you may end up becoming a source of harassment to him or her. The Bible clearly forbids that.

One sure way to ruin your child forever is to withhold the necessary chastisements. The problem with many fathers is that they know that they are unqualified to be fathers. They often take out this frustration upon their children. Some mothers also do this same thing. They possess no information on fatherhood at all. They are ill-prepared for the job.

Now, such parents must count daily upon the wisdom derived from the Book of books--the Bible. It says: "Withhold not correction from the child: for if thou beatest him with the rod, he shall not die. Thou shalt beat him with the rod, and shalt deliver his soul from hell" (Prov. 23:13-14).

Before I am accused of encouraging child abuse, let me reiterate that I am citing the Scriptures. We can reject it or misinterpret it, but we cannot change it. I have conducted Sunday School classes on parental discipline and am open to lecture anywhere upon this vital subject.

A Father's Responsibility to His Relatives

I have already covered much of the ground on this section. But I want to direct a father's attention to the following Scriptures: I Tim. 5:7-8; II Thess. 3:6-12; I Cor. 10:24; Phil. 2:21 and 3:19.

According to the Scriptures, if a man fails to provide for his relatives, especially to members of his immediate family, he is worse than an infidel. He is no Christian at all.

This means that we must debunk the contemporary, Western individualism and me-ism which often hinders us from caring for some members of our family. Me-ism has no place in the Christian family and Christian ethics. In addition to the admonition to care for our own, the Bible has much to say about the disadvantaged and the poor.

Dr. Stephen Olford, the dean of American preachers, describes a father's responsibilities in terms of the sacrifices, spirituality, and the saviorhood in the home. He says that a father must be a prophet, priest and king in the home.[7]

Are you a prophet, a priest and a king in your home? Do you have a family altar where the family meets regularly to talk with God? Do you wake up early in the morning to lead the family prayers? Or, do you wake up with curses on your lips? A family that prays together stays together, it is often said. As a father, you must try this, too.

You may now ask, "Why do you place so much emphasis upon the spiritual aspect of fatherhood?" The answer is simple. Without it, a father soon becomes a tyrant in the home. Already, some fathers and husbands have become tyrants in their homes. There is no democracy in such homes. Do you not know of some neighbors who wake up fighting and go to bed fighting? There is no peace. They fight like cats and dogs constantly.

The spiritual emphasis has been neglected by the family experts for too long. Have their prescriptions worked? Maybe. But I am offering what is working for me and my family. I am sharing the word of God. Since God is my helper, I can count on Him to help me be a good and godly father. Our God is a good God.

God is also a well-disciplined being. He is willing to aid us in this area of the human experience. This, then, is the biblical style of fatherhood which God demands and which society desperately needs. If we are responsible to ourselves, our wives, our children, our relatives, and our God, we cannot fail in this holy calling.

4

THE FOUR REWARDS
OF FATHERHOOD

You may recall Bill Cosby's joke that fatherhood is like asking your child to conceal his or her parental identity.

I should assure you that fatherhood is not altogether negative. It has its rewards.[1] Keep in mind the old adage: "Like father, like son." There are four wonderful rewards for those who succeed as fathers.

Indescribable Joy

On this earth, successful fathers have the indescribable joy of parenting. Those who have been fathers already know what I am saying. During the 1992-1993 school year, I was away from my family for the year. I was only able to visit them from New Orleans for a few days each semester.

I cannot believe the loneliness which I felt from being separated from my wife and daughter. I had large telephone bills as a result of communication across country. There is joy in watching your child grow up from a tiny baby to a toddler, then to a teenager, and finally to a full-grown man or woman.

God has put this joy in our hearts. When a child does not turn out right, a parent's heart is often broken. This aspect of fulfillment from child-rearing flies in the face of the lesbian/homosexual ideology. If all these homosexuals really meant business, how do they hope to find this kind of joy when they cannot produce children from partners of the same gender? From purely a biological point of view, it is impossible for them unless they hope to adopt the children of "straight" men and women. Fathering (and mothering) provide us with a real source of self-actualization.

Society Is Made Better

Our success as fathers affects the success of any community and society. Our society is the better for having good fathers. All the problems associated with any society are linked with the family and with the kind of fathers which that society produces.

Studies have shown that fathers have direct impact upon their sons and daughters. John F. Kennedy and Martin Luther King, Jr. were greatly affected by their fathers. What a difference the history of the 20th Century would have been had Adolf Hitler's father influenced his son for good![2] Unfortunately, today, we all tend to blame the government for all our social troubles, whereas the solution lies in our willingness to reform the family. We must confess our sins and failure as fathers, and repent.

A Soul-Winner's Crown

Since fathers must reproduce their spiritual kind, there is a divine recompense for those fathers who raise up Christian children. Every child born into this world comes as a sinner. Your first evangelistic task must be the salvation of your child. This is why my wife and I began to pray for our children even before they were conceived. We have been praying for them ever since and have not stopped. What about you?

Fathers (and mothers) who lead their children to Christ have the promise of a soul-winner's crown (I Thess. 2:19). In addition, there is a crown of glory (I Pet. 5:4) for them as redeemed people and a crown of gold (Rev. 4:4) for excellent work for their Master. For the magnificent work of winning your children to Christ, there is a reward.

We should not pretend to be unaware that there are social costs for sin. Every time, therefore, that a child or anyone else is made to become a real Christian, the society gains. The government also gains. Everybody gains from the benefits of righteous living. But sin is a reproach to any people (Prov. 14:34).

Family Tradition and Family Pride

Successful fathers can initiate a family tradition and pride. Nothing gives a young person such a sense of pride and confidence as knowing that he or she comes from a long line of great ancestors. But, to achieve this, a father must start at some point.

As you read this, maybe you are saying to yourself, "My family name is insignificant. I am nobody." Even this kind of thought is significant because you already know something about yourself which you can change.

Believe me, you are somebody. You are God's own unique creation. You are considered great in His sight. With hard work, perseverance and dedication, you too can be great. You can achieve the unthinkable.

Think of Jesse Jackson and his family background. As a fatherless child, what chance did he have to be known in America someday as a black presidential candidate?

Think of John H. Johnson, the publisher of *Ebony* magazine. What chance did he have in 1945 to become a great name in America?

Nobody ever thought that Abraham Lincoln would one day become a great American president. Nobody ever thought that Albert Einstein would amount to anything. But he did.

Read the biographies of Thomas Edison, John D. Rockefeller, Andrew Carnegie, Julius Ceasar, Napoleon Bonaparte, Ludwig Beethoven, Charles Dickens, Isaac Newton, and so on. Did you know that Dickens was a lame man? Did you know that Einstein was considered unlikely to succeed?[3] Cheer up!

If you have a great dream, and, like king David of old, you cannot fulfill that dream during your life time, pass it on to your children. This is how family traditions are made. David passed on his dream to build the greatest temple for God to his son, Solomon.

You, too, can succeed with your children. Right now, you may be setting the stage for what may become the greatest tradition and heritage for your family. Your great, great grandchildren and posterity will be proud of you.

God is watching your efforts. He is interested in your success. He wants you to succeed with your children. As the communicator of His word to you, I assure you that help is there for you. Rise up and be the kind of successful father God intended you to be. With His help and guidance, you can do it!

END NOTES

Foreword

1. William Reynolds, <u>The American Father: A New Approach to Understanding Himself, His Woman, His Child</u> (NY: Paddington Press, 1978), p. 9.

2. Nancy R. Gibbs, "Bringing Up Father," <u>Time</u> 141 (June 28, 1993), pp. 52-53.

3. For more discussions about Dr. Etuk's religious background, see his book: <u>A Walk through the Wilderness</u> (NY: Carlton Press, 1990), pp.13-40.

4. Cited in Gibbs, p. 53.

5. Ken R. Canfield, <u>The Seven Secrets of Effective Fathers</u> (Wheaton, IL: Tyndale House Publishers, 1992), p. 203.

6. Cited in an editorial titled, "The Black Family Nobody Knows," <u>Ebony</u> 48 (August, 1993), p. 30.

Surprisingly, this article maintains a positive view about the condition of the black family at a time when many American families are ending up in the divorce courts.

7. See Gibbs, p. 56.

Introduction

1. Bill Cosby, <u>Fatherhood</u> (NY: Doubleday and Co., 1986), p. 15.

2. George Herbert cited in Gerald F. Lieberman, <u>3,500 Good Quotes for Speakers</u> (NY: Doubleday and Co., 1983), p. 94.

3. Cosby, <u>Fatherhood</u>, p. 96. See also Dallas, Jr., "The Meaning of Fatherhood," in Lee N. June and Matthew Parker, eds. <u>Men To Men: Perspectives of Sixteen African-American Christian Men</u> (Grand Rapids, MI: Zondervan Publishing House, 1996), pp. 129-147.

4. Cosby, <u>Fatherhood</u>., p. 18.

5. Ibid., p. 15.

6. James Patterson and Peter Kim, <u>The Day America Told the Truth: What People Really Believe About Everything That Really Matters</u> (NY: Prentice-Hall Press, 1991), p. 6.

7. "A World Without Fathers: The Struggle to Save the Black Family," <u>Newsweek</u> 122 (August 30, 1993), pp. 3, 16-29.

8. Ibid., p. 17. For recent works on the state of the American family, see Reuven Bar-Levav, <u>Every Family Needs a C.E.O.: What Mothers And Fathers Can Do About Our Deteriorating Families and Values</u> (New York: Fathering Inc., 1995), Ruth Westheimer and Ben Yagoda, <u>The Value of Family: A Blueprint For the 21st Century</u> (New York: Warner Books, 1996), and Maggie Gallagher, <u>The Abolition of Marriage: How We Destroy Lasting Love</u> (Washington, DC: Regnery Publishing, 1996).

9. "A World Without Fathers," p. 17.

10. Patterson and Kim, p. 72.

11. The Oprah Winfrey Show Telecast, June 8, 1992. Compare this with Richard Majors and Janet Mancini Billson, <u>Cool Pose: The Dilemmas of Black Manhood in America</u> (NY: Simon and Schuster, 1992), pp. 16-17.

Compare this also with Glenda Riley, <u>Divorce: An American Tradition</u> (NY: Oxford University Press, 1991), pp. 156-181.

12. Patterson and Kim, p. 84.

13. Ibid., p. 71.

14. Canfield, <u>The Seven Secrets of Effective Fathers</u>, p. 197.

Chapter 2

1. William S. Beck, "Human Body," in <u>The Encyclopedia Americana</u>, vol. 14 (Danbury, CT: Grolier, Inc., 1991), p. 547.

2. Rhonda Harrington Kelley, <u>Divine Discipline: How to Develop and Maintain Self-Control</u> (Gretna, LA: Pelican Publishing Co., 1992), pp. 31-51, 105-115

offers one of the best expositions on the meaning and practice of personal discipline.

See also Richard J. Foster, <u>Celebration of Discipline: The Path to Spiritual Growth</u>, revised edition (NY: HarperCollins Publishers, 1988).

3. See the "Special Report" in <u>Details</u>, 12 (June 1993), pp. 82-89.

See also another special report titled, "Sex for Sale: An Alarming Boom in Prostitution Debases the Women and Children of the World," <u>Time</u>, 141 (June 21, 1993), pp. 44-51, 52-55.

See also <u>Newsweek</u>, (June 21, 1993), pp. 54-60 which has a special feature on lesbians "coming out strong."

4. Majors and Billson, <u>Cool Pose</u>, p. 31.

Chapter 3

1. Lewis Yablonsky, <u>Fathers and Sons</u> (NY: Simon and Schuster, 1982), p. 13.

2. Edwin Louis Cole, <u>Communication, Sex and Money</u> (Tulsa, OK: Harrison House, Inc., 1987), p. 17.

3. Ibid., p. 25.

4. See Augustine B. Nsamenang, "A West African Perspective," in Michael E. Lamb, ed., <u>The Father's Role: Cross-Cultural Perspectives</u> (Hillsdale, NJ: Lawrence Erlbaum Associates, Publishers, 1987), pp. 273-293.

5. Matthew N. O. Sadiku, <u>Secrets of Successful Marriages</u> (Philadelphia, PA: Covenant Publishers, 1991), pp. 331-333.

6. Bill Cosby alludes to this in <u>Fatherhood,</u> p. 41.

7. Stephen Olford in his Encounter Ministry Radio broadcast over Radio ELWA on September 5, 1976.

Chapter 4

1. Canfield, <u>The Seven Secrets of Effective Fathers,</u> pp. 10-13.

2. See Victor Goertzel and Mildred G. Goertzel, <u>Cradles of Eminence</u> (Boston, MA; Little Brown and Co., 1962).

3. See John C. Maxwell, <u>Developing the Leader Within You</u> (Nashville, TN: Thomas Nelson Publishers, 1993), p. 131, and John W. Gardner, <u>On Leadership</u> (NY: The Free Press, 1990), pp. 162-170.

SELECTED BIBLIOGRAPHY

'Abd al 'Ati, Hammudah. The Family Structure in Islam. Brentwood, MD: American Trust Publications, 1977.

Appleton, William S. Fathers and Daughters: A Father's Powerful Influence on a Woman's Life. NY: Doubleday and Co., 1981.

Bakan, David. And They Took Them Wives: The Emergence of Patriarchy in Western Civilization. San Francisco, CA: Harper and Row, 1979.

Beer, William R. Househusbands: Men and Housework in American Families. NY: Praeger Publishers, 1983.

Benson, Leonard. Fatherhood: A Sociological Perspective. NY: Random House, 1968.

Berman, Phyllis W. and Pedersen, Frank A., eds. Men's Transitions to Parenthood: Longitudinal Studies of Early Family Experience. Hillsdale, NJ: Lawrence Erlbaum Associates, Publishers, 1987.

Billingsley, Andrew. <u>Climbing Jacob's Ladder: The Enduring Legacy of African-American Families</u>. NY: Simon and Schuster, 1992.

Bloom, Allan. <u>Love and Friendship</u>. NY: Simon and Schuster, 1993.

Boose, Lynda E. and Flowers, Betty S., eds. <u>Daughters and Fathers</u>. Baltimore, MD: The Johns Hopkins University Press, 1989.

Butler, Sandra. <u>Conspiracy of Silence: The Trauma of Incest</u>. San Francisco, CA: Volcano Press, 1985.

Canfield, Ken R. <u>The 7 Secrets of Effective Fathers</u>. Wheaton, IL: Tyndale House Pubishers, 1992.

Carey, Art. <u>In Defense of Marriage</u>. NY: Walker and Co., 1984.

Cath, Stanley H., Gurwitt, Alan R., and Ross, John Munder, eds., <u>Father and Child: Developmental and Clinical Perspectives</u>. Boston, MA: Little, Brown and Co., 1982.

Cole, Edwin Louis, <u>Communication, Sex and Money</u>. Tulsa, OK: Harrison House, Inc., 1987.

Cole, Edwin Louis, <u>Maximized Manhood: A Guide to Family Survival</u>. Springdale, PA: Whitaker House, 1982.

Colman, Arthur and Libby. <u>Earth Father/Sky Father: The Changing Concept of Fathering</u>. Englewood Cliffs, NJ: Prentice-Hall, 1981.

Cosby, Bill. <u>Childhood</u>. NY: G. P. Putnam's Sons, 1991.

Cosby, Bill. <u>Love and Marriage</u>. NY: Doubleday and Co., 1989.

Cosby, Bill. <u>Fatherhood</u>. NY: Doubleday and Co., 1986.

Dallas, Jr., Claude L. "The Meaning of Fatherhood." June, Lee N. and Parker, Matthew, eds., <u>Men to Men: Perspectives of Sixteen African-American Christian Men</u>. Grand Rapids, MI: Zondervan Publishing House, 1996.

Dash, Leon. <u>When Children Want Children: The Urban Crisis of Teenage Childbearing</u>. NY: William Morrow and Co., 1989.

David, Jay and Harrington, Helise, eds. <u>Growing Up African</u>. NY: William Morrow and Co., 1971.

Elster, Arthur B. and Lamb, Michael E., eds. <u>Adolescent Fatherhood</u>. Hillsdale, NJ: Lawrence Erlbaum Associates, Publishers, 1986.

Etuk, Emma S. <u>A Walk Through the Wilderness</u>. NY: Carlton Press, 1990.

Gardner, John W. <u>On Leadership</u>. NY: The Free Press, 1990.

Gibbs, Jewelle Taylor, ed. <u>Young, Black and Male in America: An Endangered Species</u>. NY: Auburn House, 1988.

Goertzel, Victor and Goertzel, Mildred G. <u>Cradles of Eminence</u>. Boston, MA: Little, Brown and Co., 1962.

Greenberg, Martin. <u>The Birth of a Father</u>. NY: Continuum, 1985.

Greif, Geoffrey L. <u>Single Fathers</u>. Lexington, MA: D. C. Heath and Co., 1985.

Greif, Geoffrey L. The Daddy Track and the Single Father. Lexington, MA: D. C. Heath and Co., 1990.

Hamilton, Marshall L. Father's Influence on Children. Chicago, IL: Nelson-Hall, 1977.

Jewell, K. Sue. Survival of the Black Family: The Institutional Impact of U.S. Social Policy. NY: Praeger, 1988.

Kelley, Rhonda Harrington. Divine Discipline: How to Develop and Maintain Self-Control. Gretna, LA: Pelican Publishing Co., 1992.

Klagsbrun, Francine. Married People: Staying Together in the Age of Divorce. NY: Bantam, 1985.

LaHaye, Tim. The Battle for the Family. Old Tappan, NJ: Fleming H. Revell Co., 1982.

Lamb, Michael E., ed. The Father's Role: Cross-Cultural Perspectives. Hillsdale, NJ: Lawrence Erlbaum Associates, Publishers, 1987.

Levitan, Sar A., Belous, Richard S. and Gallo, Frank. What's Happening to the American Family?:

Tensions, Hopes, Realities. Baltimore, MD: The Johns Hopkins University Press, 1988.

Lewis, Charlie. Becoming a Father. Philadelphia, PA: Open University Press, 1986.

Madhubuti, Haki R. Black Men: Obsolete, Single, Dangerous? Afrikan American Families in Transition: Essays in Discovery, Solution and Hope. Chicago, IL: Third World Press, 1990.

Maine, Margo. Father Hunger: Fathers, Daughters and Food. Carlsbad, CA: Gurze Books, 1991.

Majors, Richard and Billson, Janet Mancini. Cool Pose: The Dilemmas of Black Manhood in America. NY: Simon and Schuster, 1992.

Maxwell, John C. Developing the Leader Within You. Nashville, TN: Thomas Nelson Publishers, 1993.

McKee. Lorna and O'Brien, Margaret, eds. The Father Figure. London: Tavistock Publications, 1982.

Patterson, James and Kim, Peter. The Day America Told the Truth: What People Really Believe About

Everything that Really Matters. NY: Prentice-Hall Press, 1991.

Pearsall, Paul. The Power of the Family: Strength, Comfort and Healing. NY: Doubleday and Co., 1990.

Pennetti, Michael. Coping with Schoolage Fatherhood. NY: The Rosen Publishing Group, 1987.

Possner, Richard A. Sex and Reason. Cambridge, MA: Harvard University Press, 1992.

Pruett, Kyle D. The Nurturing Father: Journey Toward the Complete Man. NY: Warner Books, 1987.

Reynolds, William. The American Father: A New Approach to Understanding Himself, His Woman, His Child. NY: Paddington Press, 1978.

Riley, Glenda. Divorce: An American Tradition. NY: Oxford University Press, 1991.

Roberts, Nickie. Whores in History: Prostitution in Western Society. London: HarperCollins, 1992.

Robinson, Bryan E. Teenage Fathers. Lexington, MA: D.C. Heath and Co., 1988.

Rosenthal, Kristine M. and Keshet, Harry F. Fathers Without Partners: A Study of Fathers and the Family After Marital Separation. Totowa, NJ: Rowman and Littlefield, 1981.

Rotundo, E. Anthony. American Manhood: Transformations in Masculinity From the Revolution to the Modern Era. NY: Basic Books, 1993.

Sadiku, Matthew N. O. Secrets of Successful Marriages. Philadelphia, PA: Covenant Publishers, 1991.

Schmookler, Andrew Bard. Fool's Gold: The Fate of Values in a World of Goods. NY: HarperCollins, 1993.

Shapiro, Jerrold Lee. The Measure of a Man: Becoming the Father You Wish Your Father Had Been. NY: The Berkley Publishing Co., 1993.

Staples, Robert. The Black Family: Essays and Studies. Belmont, CA: Wadsworth Publishing Co., 1991.

Woolfolk, William. <u>Daddy's Little Girl: The Unspoken Bargain Between Fathers and Their Daughters</u>. Englewood Cliffs, NJ: Prentice-Hall, 1982.

Worth, Cecilia. <u>The Birth of a Father: New Fathers Talk about Pregnancy, Childbirth, and the First Three Months</u>. NY: McGraw-Hill Book Co., 1988.

Yablonsky, Lewis. <u>Fathers and Sons</u>. NY: Simon and Schuster, 1982.

ABOUT THE AUTHOR

Emma S. Etuk, author, speaker and historian, is the founder of Nigeria for Christ Ministries. A graduate of Howard University in Washington, DC, he obtained a Ph.D. in United States History, with minors in African History and International Relations.

Formerly a civil servant, Etuk attended the Polytechnic, Calabar, in Nigeria, where he received a Higher National Diploma in Estate Management. He also received a B. A. in Business Administration from Malone College, Canton, Ohio; M.A. in Church History from Ashland Theological Seminary; and did further graduate work at the Institute of Church and State at Baylor University in Waco, Texas.

A motivational speaker, Etuk has taught history at Howard University and Dillard University, lectured widely in Nigeria and in the United States, and has written several books, articles and essays which have been widely read. He teaches Sunday School at the Church of the Living God, in Hyattsville, Maryland, and conducts seminars and lectures on evangelism and soul-winning techniques.

He is married with two children.

BY THE SAME AUTHOR

Go Ye Out, 1979.

Destiny Is Not a Matter of Chance: Essays in Reflection and Contemplation on the Destiny of Blacks, 1989.

A Walk through the Wilderness, 1990.

SELECTED ORGANIZATIONS RELATED TO MEN AND FATHERHOOD ISSUES

1. Center on Fathering
325 N. El Paso St.
Colorado Springs, CO 80903
Tel: 800-MY DAD 34
719-634-7797
Fax: 719-634-7852

2. American Men's Studies Assn
222 East St.
Northampton, MA 01060

3. Coalition for the Preservation of Fatherhood
P.O. Box 8051
Boston, MA 02113
Tel: 617-649-1906

4. Dads Against Discrimination
Victor Smith
P.O. Box 8525
Portland, OR 97207
Tel: 503-222-1111

5. Dads Against Discrimination
Bob Karls
506 Second Ave.
Smith Tower, Ste. 1518
Seattle, WA 98104-2311
Fax: 206-623-2017

6. Dads Against Discrimination
Pat Chandler
12301 Manitoba NE
Albuquerque, NM 87111
Tel: 505-299-2673

Dad the Family Shepherd
Norman Hoggard
P.O. Box 21445
Little Rock, AR 72221
Tel: 501-221-1102

8. Dear Dad
3135 Fourth St.
Boulder, CO 80304
Tel: 800-DEAR-DAD

9. D.C. Men Against Rape
c/o Washington Peace Ctr.

2111 Florida Ave. NW
Washington, DC 20008
Tel: 202-882-5898

10. Family University
Paul Lewis, President
P.O. Box 270616
San Diego, Canada 92198
Tel: 619-487-7099

11. Father and Son Survival
c/o Journey's Together
P.O. Box 2615
Sedonia, AZ 86336

12. The Fatherhood Project
Bank Street College
610 W. 112 St.
New York, NY 10025

13. FatherNet
12 McNeal Hall
1985 Buford Ave.
Univ. of MN
St. Paul, MN 55108
Tel: 718-494-1719

14. Fathers and Children Equality
P.O. Box 117
Drexel, PA 19026
Hotline: 215-688-4748

15. Fathers Are Capable Too!
David Foster
1995 Weston Rd.
Box 79513, Weston
Ontario, CA, M9 N3 W9
Tel: 905-459-7970

16. Fathers Are Parents, Too!
Ande Burke
P.O. Box 704
Winterville, GA 30683
Tel: 404-880-KIDS

17. Fathers Behind Bars, Inc.
525 Superior St.
Niles, MI 49120

18. The Fathers' Ctr.
120 W. Lancaster Ave.
Ardmore, PA 10993
Tel: 215-644-6400

19. Fathers For Equal Rights
Adolph Riebenack
2517 Birchfield Dr., NW
Huntsville, AL 35810

20. The Fathers' Forum
The Elizabeth Bing Center for Parents
164 W. 679th St.
New York, NY 10024

21. Fathers' Resource Ctr.
430 Oak Grove St., Ste. B3
Minneapolis, MN 55403
Voicephone: 612-874-1509

22. Fathers' Rights and Equality Exchange
(F.R.E.E.)
701 Welch Rd., #323
Palo Alto, CA 94304
Tel: 415-853-6877

23. Fathers' Rights Newsline
P.O. Box 713
Havertown, PA 19083
Tel: 215-879-4099

24. Fathers United for Equal Justice
P.O. Box 1308
Nashua, NH 03061
Tel: 603-808-9389

25. The Institute for Responsible Fatherhood
and Family Revitalization
I.R.F.F.R.
Stacie Banks Hall
Tel: 202-789-6376; 216-791-8336
Pager: 800-601-4609
Fax: 216-791-0104

26. Joint Custody Assn
James A. Cook, President
10606 Wilkins Ave.
Los Angeles, CA 90024
Tel: 213-475-5352

27. Men Assisting, Leading and Educating
(M.A.L.E.)
P.O. Box 460171
Aurora, CO 8004-01716
Tel: 303-693-9930; 800-949-MALE

28. Men Against Domestic Violence
32 W. Anapamu St., #348
Santa Barbara, CA 93101
Voicemail: 805-563-2651

29. Men Stopping Violence
1020 DeKalb Ave., #25
Atlanta, GA 30307
Tel: 404-688-1376

30. Men's Defense Assn.
Richard F. Doyle, Director
17854 Lyons St.
Forest Lake, MN 55025

31. Men's Action Network
Anthony Nazzaro, Executive Director
P.O. Box 645
Dobbs Ferry, NY 10522
Tel: 914-693-7826

32. Men' Rights, Inc.
P.O. Box 163180
Sacramento, CA 95816
Tel: 916-484-7333

33. Ministry to Men, Inc.
Tom Batchelor
3931 Homewood Rd., Ste. B.
Memphis, TN 38118
Tel: 901-362-3353

34. National Assn. for Fathers (N.A.F.)
Bob Hassler
1075-D N. Railroad Ave., #111
Richmond, NY 10306
Tel: 800-HELP-DAD
BBS 718-494-1719

35. National Center For Fathering
10200 W. 75th Ave., Ste. 267
Shawnee, KS 66204
Tel: 800-593-DADS

36. National Center for Men
P.O. Box 555
Old Bethpage, NY 11804
Tel: 516-942-2020

37. National Congress for Fathers and Children
851 Minnesota Ave.

P.O. Box 171675
Kansas City, KS 66117
Tel: 800-SEE-DADS

38. National Congress for Men
210 7th St. SE
Washington, DC 20003

39. National Organization of Dads
and Kids, Inc.
Ron Roberson, President
50 Janis Way
Scotts Valley, CA 95066
Voicemail: 408-438-6658
Fax: 408-438-1257

40. National Organization for Men, Inc.
Eleven Park Place
New York, NY 10007
Tel: 212-766-4030

41. Orlando Men's Council
Jim Bracewell
P.O. Box 462
Winter Park, FL 32790
Tel: 407-629-5868

42. Promise Keepers
P.O. Box 103001
Denver, CO 80250-3001
Tel: 800-239-7028

43. Single Fathers Research Project
2901 Jefferson Dr.
Greenville, NC 27834

44. Society for the Preservation
of Family Relationships
c/o 172 Berlin Dr.
Knoxville, TN 37923

45. Texas Fathers' Alliance
807 Brazos, Ste. 315
Austin, TX 78701
Tel: 512-472-3237

46. Texas Men's Institute
Marvin Allen, Director
P.O. Box 311384
New Braunfels, TX 78131
Tel: 210-608-9201

47. Worldwide Christian Divorced Fathers
Divorce without Court
1429 Columbia Dr., NE
Albuquerque, NM 81706
Tel: 800-MY-DADDY

SELECTED INTERNET WEBSITES RELATED TO MEN AND FATHERHOOD ISSUES

1. American Father's Coalition
http://www.vix.com/pub/men/orgs/afc.html

2. Fathers' Rights and Equality Exchange
http://www.vix.com/free/index.html

3. Men's Health Network and
Men's/Fathers' Hotline
http://www.vix.com/pub/men/orgs/writeups/
menshealthnetwork.html

4. National Center for Fathering
http://www.fathers.com/

5. National Fatherhood Initiative
http://www.register.com/father/

6. Parents' Place
http://www.parentsplace.com/

7. Fatherhood Project
http://www.fatherhoodproject.org/

8. National Practitioners Network for
Fathers and Families
http://www.fatherhoodproject.org/npnpage.htm

9. Men's Issues Page
http://www.vix.com/pub/men/index.html

10. American Fathers' Coalition
http://www.erols.com/afc/

11. American Coalition for Fathers and Children
http://www.acfc.org/

12. Center on Fathering
http://www.vix.com/pub/men/orgs/blurb/
cof.html

13. Coalition for the Preservation of Fatherhood
http://www.tiac.net/users/sbasile/CPF/

14. Dads Against Discrimination (DADS)
http://www.vix.com/pub/men/orgs/blurb/
dads.html

15. Fathers for Equal Rights
http://www.vix.com/pub/men/orgs/writeups/
fer.html

16. Focus - Fathers' Rights Group
http://www.cc.utah.edu/-jv2316/focus.html

17. Men Against Domestic Abuse
http://www.silcom.com/-paladin/madv/

18. Men's Defense Association
http://www.mensdefense.org/

19. Dads Against Discrimination
http://www.teleport.com/-dads/

20. Men's Media Network
http://www.menmedia.org/

21. United Fathers of America
http://www.ufa.org/

22. Men's Resource Center
http://www.libertynet.org:80/-mrc/

23. National Coalition of Free Men
http://www.ncfm.org/

24. Real Men
http://www.cs.utk.edu/-bartley/other/real
Men.html

25 Men Related Periodicals
http://www.vix.com/pub/men/orgs/
periodicals.html#fattime

26. At-Home Dad Newsletter
http://www.parentsplace.com/readroom/
athomedad/newslett.html

27. A Man's Life Magazine
http://www.manslife.com/

28. MenWeb Magazine
http://www.vix.com/menmag/msn.html

29. Credenda Magazine: Covenant Masculinity-
The Meaning of Headship
http://www.moscow.com/Resources/Credenda/
issues/conts7-5.htm

30. Fathering Magazine
http://www.fathermag.com/

31. Family Guardian Journal
http://www.vix.com/pub/men/orgs/
writeups/family.guard.html

Order your copies now by completing the form below.

● ●

Please rush me_____ copies of *Fatherhood* @ $7.95 ea.
+ $1.50 for postage and handling
(MD residents add $.50 sales tax)

Enclosed is my Money Order for $_____ total.
(No checks please.)

Name: _____

Address: _____

City/State/Zip: _____

Make Money Orders payable to:

Dr. E. S. Etuk
P.O. Box 50317
Washington, DC 20091

Allow 4-6 weeks for delivery.